## DATE DUE

| JUL 06 '94 | | | |
|---|---|---|---|
| | | | |
| | | | |
| | | | |
| | | | |
| | | | |
| | | | |
| | | | |
| | | | |
| | | | |
| | | | |
| | | | |
| | | | |
| | | | |
| | | | |
| | | | |
| | | | |

ANCE

# BROWN

## PHYSICAL EDUCATION ACTIVITIES SERIES

Consulting Editor:

AILEENE LOCKHART
University of Southern California
Los Angeles, California

Evaluation Materials Editor:

JANE A. MOTT
Smith College
Northampton, Massachusetts

ARCHERY, Wayne C. McKinney
BADMINTON, Margaret Varner
BIOPHYSICAL VALUES OF MUSCULAR ACTIVITY, E. C. Davis,
    Gene A. Logan, and Wayne C. McKinney
BOWLING, Joan Martin
CIRCUIT TRAINING, Robert P. Sorani
CONDITIONING AND BASIC MOVEMENT CONCEPTS, Jane A. Mott
CONTEMPORARY SQUARE DANCE, Patricia A. Phillips
FENCING, Muriel Bower and Torao Mori
FIELD HOCKEY, Anne Delano
FIGURE SKATING, Marion Proctor
FOLK DANCE, Lois Ellfeldt
GOLF, Virginia L. Nance and E. C. Davis
HANDBALL, Michael Yessis
JUDO, Daeshik Kim
LACROSSE FOR GIRLS AND WOMEN, Anne Delano
BASKETBALL FOR MEN, Glenn Wilkes
GYMNASTICS FOR MEN, A. Bruce Frederick
MODERN DANCE, Esther E. Pease
PHYSICAL AND PHYSIOLOGICAL CONDITIONING FOR MEN, Benjamin Ricci
SKIING, Clayne Jensen and Karl Tucker
SKIN AND SCUBA DIVING, Albert A. Tillman
SOCCER, Richard L. Nelson
SOCIAL DANCE, William F. Pillich
SOFTBALL, Martin E. Kneer and Charles L. McCord
SQUASH RACQUETS, Margaret Varner and Norman Bramall
SWIMMING, Betty J. Vickers and William J. Vincent
TABLE TENNIS, Margaret Varner and J. R. Harrison
TAP DANCE, Barbara Nash
TENNIS, Joan Johnson and Paul Xanthos
TRACK AND FIELD, Kenneth E. Foreman and Virginia L. Husted
TRAMPOLINING, Jeff T. Hennessy
VOLLEYBALL, Glen H. Egstrom and Frances Schaafsma
WEIGHT TRAINING, Philip J. Rasch
BASKETBALL FOR WOMEN, Frances Schaafsma
GYMNASTICS FOR WOMEN, A. Bruce Frederick
WRESTLING, Arnold Umbach and Warren R. Johnson

PHYSICAL EDUCATION
ACTIVITIES SERIES

# TAP DANCE

BARBARA NASH

*Syracuse University*

WM. C. BROWN COMPANY PUBLISHERS
DUBUQUE, IOWA

Printed in United States of America

# Preface

This book on tap dance is dedicated to and written for all those "young at heart" people who gaily tap their toes to the syncopated beat of popular music. Although directed to the college age student, the information has no age or rank level; it could be used by young or old, student or instructor. The material is so fundamental, however, that it is intended chiefly for the beginner who should be learning basic movement and compositional skills. This is not a book of dances. Rather, it is an attempt to analyze the ingredients of a tap dance, to show how these are illustrated in a dance, and to encourage the student to use tap techniques as a creative dance medium.

Evaluation questions and problems are included to start the beginner on his own inventive path. Because they are designed to stimulate a creative approach to learning, the problems given are representative of the kinds of understandings and skills the reader should be developing, and, therefore, are not meant to be complete. The learner should not only answer the printed questions and develop the skills indicated but should also pose additional ones for himself. If he finds he cannot respond completely or precisely, he should review his skills before attempting more difficult ones. But enough of talk. Let's go. Read. Tap it out. Enjoy yourself. You are on the way!

# Contents

# What Is
# Tap Dance Like?

What is this thing called tap dance? It is dancing, dancing with the toes. It is joyous, vital, noisy, vigorous, expressive, rhythmic action; it is fun to do, fun to watch. Though it gives the impression of spontaneous expression, it is carefully ordered. It may be serious, comical, satirical, interpretive; it usually entertains—it is a form of dancing.

Use of the feet sets tap dancing apart from other forms of dance and gives it a special appeal. When you watch most dances, you see but do not hear the rhythmic patterns. You hear the musical accompaniment and relate sight and sound patterns. In tap dancing you not only see but you also hear the rhythmic patterns produced by the movement of the feet. Even if no accompaniment is used, there is a sound pattern. With musical accompaniment, both dancer and audience are conscious of the interplay of the two aural rhythms. This is the charm and the appeal of tap dancing.

The primary sound-producing agent is the foot. To augment the sound, a shoe with a metal plate at toe and at the heel is worn. These are the "taps." The attention of the audience is directed to the music produced by the dancer's feet. Excitement for the audience comes from the speed and complexity of patterns, the syncopation of sounds, and the style of performance. Excitement for the dancer comes from the mastery of aural physical skills, the pleasure of not only feeling but of hearing what is right. The slurred, missed, or hesitant tap sound is obvious. The dancer has a real feeling of accomplishment when the first dance is done perfectly or when a complicated sequence is mastered. There is an obvious right and wrong. This does not imply that there is no right and wrong in other forms of dance. There is a perfection of technique and mastery of a particular movement sequence in any form of dance, but in tap the close coordination of sound and movement with accompaniment makes the dancer more conscious of errors.

Who can learn to tap? Anyone who can walk. Is there an adult who has not at some time jigged and shuffled and tapped a toe while listening to a stimulating piece of music? Where can you learn how to tap? The professional studio has been in business since early in this century. Schools, colleges, and recreation centers offer classes in tap. For a long time, there was criticism of tap as an educational tool; educators felt that it represented only a training process, that one dance was learned, then another, then another without learning and using the techniques as a basis for individual invention or for gaining a real understanding of the elements that comprise a good dance. The fault lies not with the material but rather in the method of presentation. The studio approach customarily teaches dances to increase skills for maximum performance. The school approach, however, should be to teach dance as a means of understanding techniques and principles of composition for the creative use of the student.

There are limitations in the range of movement suitable for tap dancing. Although the total body is in action, only those patterns of leg and foot action are used in tap dancing which can produce sound or are extensions of preceding or succeeding sound patterns. The torso and arms must complement the leg actions. In modern dance, there is no limitation to the choice of movement other than that which is appropriate to content; in ballet the limitations are governed by technique and content, in modern jazz by style and content. When you have learned a minimum of basic movement actions and a few Sequences in tap, you can begin to invent your own variations and combinations of patterns. With an understanding of spatial, dynamic, rhythmic, and structural principles, you can construct simple dances that are fun to do and fun to watch. This element of fun is especially important to tap which developed historically as a form of light entertainment. The professional dancer continues to entertain in the theatre; the amateur taps for personal recreation.

# 2

# The Past

Where did tap dance come from? How did it start? Was it invented by the creative imagination of an early theatrical genius, or did it grow through the inventions of many celebrated stars and anonymous dancers? These questions are difficult to answer. It "grew like Topsy" with the growth of the popular American theatre; and yet, there was an individual who performed an act about 1830 who is recognized as the first to synthesize a peculiar style of movement into a song and dance routine. The instant popularity of the act created a demand for more of the same. From this impetus the form of dance which we now call tap grew and flourished. "Daddy" Rice did not invent a new dance. He borrowed patterns from an improvised form of dance that had been enjoyed for years by Negros in the South; he borrowed characteristic steps and postures and set them to the tune and words of "Jump Jim Crow." The shuffling foot actions, jumps, twists and turns were infectious and produced a pattering of foot sounds that accompanied the song.

Use of the foot to accent the rhythmic patterns of dance is as old as the dances of man. Curt Sachs, in *World History of the Dance*, speaks of the stamping foot as the first time beater. Even before there were Negros in the South, intricate shuffling, stamping, heel and toe actions were a part of the dance patterns of many peoples in widely separated geographical areas. In the Flamenco dances of the Gypsies, the breathtaking rapidity of the heel- and toe-beats contrasts with the sound of the castanets. The Schuhplatter dancers stamp, jump, twist, and turn, augmenting the foot sounds with slaps on leather breeches, knees, and shoe soles. In the Irish jigs and reels the ball of the foot makes rapid pattering sounds on the dance floor. The hornpipe dancers shuffle, run on the heels, click the heels in the air. In England the Lancashire clog dancers in wooden-soled shoes tap out the rhythmic patterns of the

**3**

dance. In many African tribal dances, there is shuffling, treading, and stamping of the foot in intricate rhythmic patterns.

Ethnic and folk material was available in the mid-nineteenth century. The song and dance entertainer borrowed from what he knew or what he saw; he adapted it to his purpose, and he invented new combinations to increase his repertoire. This process of borrowing, adapting, and inventing has continued to augment the movement material of tap dancing.

## PURPOSE: TO ENTERTAIN

The primary purpose of the tap dancer has always been to entertain. His place has been in the popular theatre; his audience was, until the advent of motion pictures and television, the middle and lower class rather than the elite and sophisticated segment of society. Since 1830 the interests of audiences have changed. What was popular then is now out of favor; what is popular today will probably have lost its glamour in thirty years. The need for audience appeal has produced changes in format, style, complexity, and virtuosity. To see how some of these changes have occurred, one can go back to "Daddy" Rice and the beginning of the minstrel days.

Thomas Dartmouth Rice was one of many traveling entertainers in the early nineteenth century. His claim to fame came when he presented a new act based on a song he had heard a Negro stage driver sing and the shuffling, loose-limbed, distorted dancing he had observed a Negro groom perform. He blackened his face and borrowed a porter's clothes. The catchy words and tune of "Jump Jim Crow" and the fantastic dancing which was accompanied with shoe sounds was an instant success. He was acclaimed in small towns as well as in Philadelphia, Boston, and New York. The success of this and his other similar acts even took him to England.

The song and dance that Rice presented was just one act in an evening's entertainment. Audiences expected variety, a play or two with singing and dancing in solo and ensemble as entr'actes. The dancing was likely to be ballet or folk jigs, reels, or hornpipes. It was in the entr'acte not only on the stage but also in the circuses that the comedian and the song-and-dance man in blackface showed his skill. As the number of these acts increased, two types of Negro impersonations emerged. One was patterned on the southern plantation worker, naive, good humored, unsophisticated, and costumed in tatters and patches. Jim Crow was the plantation type. The swagger of the frontiersman and the river boatman gradually mingled with the Negro characteristics. The other type was the counterpart of the white city slicker, the dandy of Broadway. His actions were sophisticated, his costume the ultra modern, often a blue coat with long tails, referred to in song as the "long tail blue." Zip Coon was a character of this type.

4

The solo banjoist began to make his mark as an entertainer. He could not play and dance, but he tapped his toe as he played and sang. In the circus ring, he performed on a raised wooden board to give greater clarity to the sound of the taps. These entertainers performed on the stages, in the circus, and in the saloons and beer halls where the audience was male, rough and hearty, ready for a laugh, and coarse in their humor.

## ACTS ENLARGE

The soloist, dancer and banjoist, joined forces to form duos, triples, and quartets. The acts enlarged as indicated by play bills listing Ethiopian Operas, Black Operas, Ethiopian Scenes—white performers in blackface. Although each dancer had his own style, the dances were characterized by large expanded angular torso movements, vigorous arm and leg movement, fairly rapid heel and toe work, sometimes called "heel and toe breakdowns" or "buck and wing." The dances appeared spontaneous but were carefully planned. The audience demanded variety and showmanship. In a short five to ten minutes, the act had to capture audience enthusiasm, make its point, and exit in a blaze of glory. Not a minute could be wasted. The dancer was expected to be humorous, have tremendous flexibility and endurance, be accomplished in speed and precision, and have a large repertoire of steps.

## EARLY DANCERS

One of the great dancers of these early days was John Diamond; the jig was his specialty. In his "Rattle Snake Jig" it is said that he performed 120 different steps. His closest rival was William Henry Lane, better known as Juba. Diamond represented the folk dance and Juba the Negro influence. The two were masters of their art.

Juba was a Negro. He learned his trade early performing in saloons and dance halls and then on the stage proper. His talent was so great that he was accepted by the white minstrels, even to the extent of touring with a white minstrel group and receiving top billing. The competition between Diamond and Juba led to challenge matches. This was a serious competitive match with strong audience partisanship. Three judges determined the winner. The Time judge sat on stage; the Style judge sat in or near the orchestra; and the Execution judge sat under the stage to check the defective sound patterns. The winner gained in reputation and acquired a purse of money. Juba was billed as the "King of All Dancers."

When Charles Dickens visited in New York City in 1842, he had an opportunity to see a Negro dancer, supposedly Juba. In his *American Notes,* he wrote "single shuffle, double shuffle, cut and cross-cut; snapping his fingers, rolling his eyes, turning in his knees, presenting the backs of his legs in front, spinning about on his toes and heels like nothing but the man's fingers on the Tambourine; dancing with two left legs, two right legs, two wooden legs, two wire legs, two spring legs—all sorts and no legs. . . ." Riding on the crest of his popularity wave, Juba went to England and joined Pell's Ethiopian Serenaders. He was billed as "Boz's Juba." His reputation had preceded him and his performances surpassed the expectation. One critic noted that he had been commanded to Buckingham Palace. His dancing was amazing; he could perform with equal dexterity both the fast and the slow steps. His competitors excelled in only one or the other. Juba's influence kept the Negro source material reasonably authentic. Both whiteface and blackface performers borrowed from his inventiveness.

The Minstrel Show was the proving ground for entertainers who tapped out their dances. It provided the frame for the blackface comedian to sing and dance and to comment on contemporary affairs. Whitlock, D. Pelham, Emmett, and Brower happened to be together in Whitlock's boarding house in New York City. All being seasoned performers and versatile in playing, singing, and dancing, they picked up their instruments—fiddle, banjo, bones, and tambourine— and started what today would be called a jam session. "Old Dan Tucker" was the lead-off tune. Pleased with their success, they planned an act and called themselves the Virginia Minstrels. Their first confirmed date was February 6, 1843, at the Bowery Amphitheatre. The four, in blackface, sat in a semicircle, the two end men with tambo and bones, the middle men with fiddle and banjo. Dressed in disreputable garments, with great hilarity and robustness, they carried on a spontaneous conversational chatter, played, sang, and the end men burst into breakdowns. Thus the Minstrel Show was born; it flourished for more than 40 years. At this early stage, there was no Mr. Interlocutor; Dan Emmett with his banjo was the leader. The Virginia Minstrels became famous and emerged as a symbol for a high standard of Minstrelsy. As the popularity of the Minstrel Show grew, the format expanded to three parts: Part I—the instrumental and vocal songs, casual banter, breakdowns, and stump speeches; Part II—the Olio, an assortment of virtuoso acts; Part III—the Southern plantation scenes and a "walk-around," a general smashing song-and-dance finale. All female roles were played by men. The tappers and eccentric dancers found a spot in all three parts. Many groups were formed. One of the early competitors of the Virginia Minstrels was the Christy Minstrels; a later top-ranking group was Bryant's Minstrels. Dan Emmett joined Bryant's and wrote "Dixie" which became a favorite for the concluding "walk-around." During the 1860's, the emphasis was placed on the Olio, the specialty acts, and then the blackface hosts of Parts I and III began to fade into history. The variety show called Vaudeville was being born.

## TAP DANCE EMERGES

Important steps had been taken in the establishment of tap as a specialized form of dance. The early style had been flamboyant, expansive, body-twisting, feet striking with heel and toe or brushing or slapping the floor, legs capering in air, arms and hands flinging up and out, complete animation with talking, laughing, and singing. The Negro material and the folk jigs, reels, and hornpipes were differentiated. By mid-century the gesticulating expansive movements were avoided. The Negro and folk elements started to merge. Actions became more sophisticated, the body elegant and balanced; action of arms and legs was easy, the feet staying close to the floor; there was more syncopated sound. This trend to smaller but faster foot and sound patterns and to polish and perfection has continued. The boisterous play gave way to sophistication. The early terminology was colorful; the names of the steps mentioned in songs are provocative—pigeon wing, jay bird wing, cutting the long J bow, turkey trot, walking jawbone, tracking on the heel, and the shuffle, double shuffle, and double trouble. Early in the century, pennies were screwed on the heels of boots to strengthen the sound. By the early 1840's, clog shoes were worn to emphasize percussive rhythms. The taps were heard as an accompaniment to the dance, sometimes called "heel solos." One entertainer was billed as a "heelologist." The Minstrel dances were usually fast, but there were also dances with a distinctive, slow tempo. By mid-century these were called "essences." Dan Bryant, of Bryant's Minstrels, was famous for his slow essence.

The Minstrel Shows were not the only kind of popular entertainment in the nineteenth century. There were Museums, Pantomimes, Extravaganzas, Circuses; the Variety Shows which played in tents, showboats, town halls, opera houses, saloons, and beer halls flourished. By wagon and later by train, the troups of singers, dancers, and actors took their entertainment to the country and the city folk. As transportation became easier, larger and more elaborate shows were presented. The whiteface and blackface song-and-dance man was a robust and popular element in all types of shows.

## EARLY VAUDEVILLE

Vaudeville, as we knew it, grew out of the Olio section of the Minstrel Show. It was Tony Pastor who put Vaudeville on its feet as a family entertainment. In 1881 he presented a "clean" show with eight acts of comedy, acrobatics, song and dance at the 14th Street Theatre to which men could take their wives and children without embarrassment. Pastor's first show was a success. Vaudeville was on its way. Keith, Proctor, and Albee capitalized on the growing popularity. The entertainment was topical, gay, never highbrow; it played to a democratic audience that wanted to laugh and wanted to be amused. The two-a-day show had many acts; if one did not please, the next one would. Each act was an independent venture, and there was no rousing finale. The last two-a-day straight show played at the Palace in New York in 1932. Motion pictures, radio, and television have replaced the live popular shows.

Vaudeville was the training ground for many who later became stars in motion pictures, radio, musical comedy, serious theatre, and television. The acts were rarely longer than ten minutes and demanded precision, polish, and absolute timing to establish the personality of the performer, to display his talents, and to move to a climax. Eddie Cantor and George Jessel were "hoofers" first; Walter Winchell for a brief time was a "hoofer" in a Gus Edwards act. George M. Cohan and family were stars before George left to produce his own shows. Irene and Vernon Castle, Pat Rooney, Fred Astaire, and the great Bill (Bojangles) Robinson danced their way to the top.

The Vaudeville show presented an ideal framework. The tap dancer emerged as a virtuoso of movement and sound. When electric lights replaced the gas lights in theatres, costumes and make-up were refined; the patent leather clog shoe became stylish. The low-heeled patent leather tie is still with us. Individual inventiveness added to the stock of material. Kitty O'Neill was one of the great sand dancers. (About the time of the Civil War, women gained acceptance as popular entertainers.) Sand was sprinkled on the front of the stage. Dancing in thin hard-soled shoes on the ball of the foot with shuffle and gliding steps, shifting and digging in the sand, the dancer produced sharp, staccato sounds. It was difficult. Not many reached the peak of Kitty's performance. The Soft Shoe developed. Eddie Leonard was an early Soft Shoe artist. Charlie Diamond danced a Soft Shoe while playing a harp. Eddie Girard was a headliner in Soft Shoe although he was also adept in the buck and wing, pointed toe, and sand jigging. He invented a new clog to the popular schottische tunes. For a while, he teamed with Willie Mahoney who was an excellent clogger. Lew Dockstader started his career dancing in pubs for "throw money" and went on to star billing in monologues, jigs, and clogs. Johnny and Bertha Gleason started as children in a brother-sister act as wooden shoe dancers. They became one of the great adult dance teams. One of their innovations was a dancing mat constructed of wood strips which made the sound of the taps sharp and clear, and it could be rolled and carried on tour. In many of the new theatres, the stage floor had no resilience which caused the tap sounds to be dull.

There was great variety in song-and-dance acts. There were impersonations of various ethnic groups—the Dutch, Irish, Jew, Swede, Negro, and the thrifty Scot. Not all blackface acts were Negro comics or impersonations; some used the blackface with no attempt to imitate the dialect or dance of the dandy or plantation worker. J. W. Andrews used a shuffling dance like a sand jig without sand and exited with a "juba," perhaps a recall of the antics of the famous Juba. A favorite act was the rival song-and-dance team. Contests between performers were held in Lancashire clog, American clog, hornpipes, trick clog, statue clog, sand jigs, and pedestal clog. Time, Style, and Execution judges determined the winner in the same fashion as in the contests between Juba and Diamond.

Although Vaudeville hit its peak between 1900 and 1920, it was not without competition from other popular entertainment. Musical Comedies and the Revues offered the dancer a prominent role. The Revue, a loosely organized structure with no central theme, relied heavily on dance routines, sketches, and musical numbers. The *Passing Shows* were annual productions for several years. Ned Wayburn made a name for himself as one of the best show dance choreographers in the *Passing Show* of 1912. In the 1913 show, he introduced the Cakewalk; the 1914 show introduced Marilyn Miller, and the slender modern chorus girl forever eclipsed the buxom beauties of an earlier time; the 1915 show revived buck and wing dancing; the 1918 show starred Fred and Adele Astaire. In the *Ziegfeld Follies,* the *Scandals,* and *Vanities,* all annual revues for a time, the tap dancer had his share of glory. Lew Leslie's *Blackbirds of 1928,* an all-Negro revue, brought Bill Robinson to Broadway and tap dancing was featured in the show. Eleven years later he starred in *The Hot Mikado,* tapping the title role. *The Band Wagon,* acclaimed as one of the best revues to hit Broadway, introduced revolving stages, and Fred Astaire danced as they revolved.

After 1930, the Revue changed, became more sophisticated, less extravagant, and moved to the smaller off-Broadway theatres. Dance moved into other mediums. The growth of mass media entertainment in motion pictures and television opened new doors to the tap dancer. The variety show continues in an altered form primarily in television programs and nightclub entertainment. Radio City Music Hall complements its picture with a stage show; the tap dancing is excellent. Gene Kelly, Ray Bolger, Fred Astaire have brought tap dance to a high level of artistry in both motion pictures and television.

Standing apart from the tap dancers in the entertainment field are Paul Draper and Agnes de Mille. Draper has used tap as a serious artistic medium presenting full length concerts with dances to Bach as well as to music of contemporary composers. Some of his sequences have been written in Labanotation and are on file at the Dance Notation Bureau. Agnes de Mille drew heavily from both square dance and tap dance material for her ballet *Rodeo.*

## TAP DANCE FOR ALL

Early in this century, tap dance studios began opening their doors to the professionals, to amateurs with dreams of the stage, and to amateurs who wished to learn just for the fun of dancing. Now, from East to West and North to South, almost every private professional studio that offers instruction in ballet also offers classes in tap—from beginning to advanced, for children or adults. Some studios specialize only in tap, or tap and modern jazz. Classes in tap were introduced into the public school and into college programs. Student interest in tap dance reached a peak in the thirties. A decline of interest in the forties was followed by a renewal of interest which has continued.

Tap dance has been part of the entertainment world for well over a hundred years. As audience demands have changed, the dance has kept the best of the past and has added an ever-increasing wealth of material to the present. As long as there are creative dancers and fresh opportunities, it seems likely that audiences will encourage the tap dancer to greater virtuosity and to the exploration of new material. The jigging, shuffling, winging feet will continue to joyfully tap their way into the future.

# 3

# Equipment

One of the splendid advantages of tap dance is that many external items are not required for learning. Tap is an activity that can be learned alone, in small groups, or in large groups. The dances learned or created can be for any number of people—one, two, three, twenty. As a group activity, all can be working on the same thing at the same time, or sub-groups can be working on individual problems. This makes possible a very flexible organization and one in which different levels of skill and expectation of accomplishment can be accommodated.

The first consideration is a room large enough to allow freedom of movement. The size of the group will determine minimum room size. The room should not be cluttered with furniture. A gymnasium, dance studio, practice room, stage, lounge, empty class room are all possible areas; the dance studio with large mirrors is an ideal location. Floor surface is the next consideration. Actually, any surface can be used if it is not slippery. To be able to hear the sound of the taps is so important that a hard surface is desirable. In order of preference, the types range from a hardwood resilient floor, tile, linoleum, concrete, to a carpeted floor. If the floor is waxed, the wax used must be of the nonskid variety.

Besides the performing area, only a source of accompaniment is necessary—a phonograph and records. In selecting records, the best for dance are those which hold a steady tempo, have marked phrasing, and are instrumental rather than vocal. Since most accompaniment will be contemporary popular music, there is little difficulty in finding appealing music.

The dancer requires comfortable clothes that allow complete freedom of the body. Leotards and tights, shorts, full skirt, slacks are appropriate. Shoes are the distinguishing essential feature. Tap shoes can be ordered from a dance supply house. Taps will be mounted on the shoes.

## EQUIPMENT

In many large towns and cities, tap shoes can be purchased in local shoe stores. If you plan to buy tap shoes, you will find several styles available —the black patent leather low-heeled tie or the higher heeled tie in black or white; most shoe stores carry only the low-heeled patent leather style. There is variety in the taps. They range from the simple small metal toe piece, the heavier broader toe piece, to the hollow toe piece with a jingle. The heel tap matches the toe tap. Taps are not expensive. The price for toe taps will range from $.50 to $2.50 a pair, and shoes are available from $6.50 to $17.95.

You do not have to buy special tap shoes. The toe and heel taps can be purchased and attached to a leather-soled shoe and removed at a later date. The local shoemaker can attach them. If you plan to attach taps to your own shoes, be sure that the sole is leather; the little nails will not hold securely in a composition sole. Be sure that the shoe fits your foot snugly and that the heel is low. If you want to attach heel taps, the heel must be fairly wide. The toe tap is essential; the heel tap is desirable. Sneakers are not a possible substitute for shoes; the rubber sole will stick to the floor and the tap nails will not hold in the rubber.

A room large enough for vigorous movement, a hard surfaced floor, music, action clothing, taps on shoes—and you are ready to begin.

# 4

# Here We Go—
# Organization of Material

Tap dance is one form of organized rhythmic movement. It is movement that is structured or planned with reference to a particular rhythmic pattern, a particular spatial pattern, and is performed with a particular style and specific dynamics. The performance of the dance results not only in enjoyment and a sense of achievement for the individuals who are dancing but also in satisfaction and entertainment for those who are watching. This is a "spectator" dance; it needs to be shared. You can play with sounds and improvise movement patterns in the privacy of your room or while waiting for a bus but you will not receive maximum satisfaction until you formalize the patterns into a complete dance and perform it for your friends. In this respect it is similar to a gymnastic or synchronized swimming skill. When you have invented or mastered a move or stunt, the approval of a friend inflates the ego and deepens your sense of achievement. The approval is more valuable if the friend, or audience, is knowledgeable about the difficulties or the intricacies of the pattern.

Improvisation is the starting point for building your own dances. But it isn't the finished product. You not only need to move freely and experimentally, but you also need to analyze what you have done so you can remember it. The most satisfactory way to make the pattern a permanent part of your dance repertoire is to write it down. After several months of disuse, memory, even motor memory, becomes faulty. With written words and symbols as a guide, a dance once learned can be easily re-learned. If you understand the written words and symbols, a new dance can be easily interpreted and new material can be added to your repertoire.

Understanding the elements is the first step in analysis. The second is learning a simple set of words and symbols in order to record; the

**13**

third is acquiring the skill to analyze what you have done; the final step is to accurately record what you have done. There are five elements that need to be understood; a complete description of a tap dance includes all these elements.

The first consideration is the movement pattern: *Movement Analysis*. These movement patterns produce the sound patterns: *Time* or *Temporal Analysis*. As you move in one place or move from one place to another, you will produce a design in space: *Space* or *Spatial Analysis*. You cannot move without exerting effort. The shapes that the body assumes and the degrees of tension, points of emphasis, and degrees of energy exerted produce a style and a dynamic pattern. Style and dynamics must relate to the purpose of the dance and its intended effect on the observer; *Content Analysis*. The way in which the various parts of the dance are joined together must not only be logical in movement, time, and space, but also must be related to content: *Structural Analysis*.

When you have considered these elements and analyzed how you have made use of them, there is one more factor to consider before making your final recording. All art forms may be judged or evaluated on the basis of certain aesthetic principles. These principles may serve as guides in structuring your movement patterns and as criteria for evaluation by the spectator. Although simple tap dances may not fall within the realm of art, still these aesthetic principles are essential in a satisfying and well constructed dance. An understanding of these principles in one medium should make possible their application to another medium; such understanding is basic to a rich appreciation of art.

When all these elements have been carefully considered and changes based on them have been made, the recording is made and your dance is then formalized, ready for your performance or for interpretation by someone else. Each of these elements will now be considered in more detail.

# 5

# What Are You Doing?
# —Movement Analysis

Movement is the medium of expression in any form of dance. In tap, chief interest lies in those patterns which produce sound. Most of the sound patterns result from the foot striking the floor. The part of the foot, the direction of the action, and the force exerted all influence the quality of the sound produced. It is possible to vary the intensity of the sound by using the foot in different ways. The sound pattern may also be augmented by making sounds with other parts of the body—like finger snapping or hand clapping, or by using a "prop" such as a cane with which to strike the floor. All of these increase interest in the total design of the movement. The foot, however, is the chief sound-producing agent. The leather-soled shoe makes a soft scuffing sound. When the metal piece (tap) has been added to the toe and heel, a sharp brittle sound results. The floor surface also influences the quality of sound; try your taps on a hardwood floor, concrete, linoleum, tile, and a carpeted floor and notice the changes in volume and timbre.

Most of the sounds are made by the toe of the shoe. Stand with the weight on your right foot and let the toe of the left foot tap the floor slowly. Increase the speed of the tapping; notice the need for good ankle flexibility as you decrease the size of the movement and increase the speed of the tapping action. Try circling the ankle, first in one direction and then the other, letting the toe touch the floor on the lowest part of each circle. A different sound is produced and you need not only flexibility of the ankle but also flexibility and control of the toe action. Clear, fast tapping sounds are produced by small movements of the foot. As control of the smaller foot patterns increases, sounds become more rapid, feet stay closer to the floor, and more intricate coordinations are possible.

Many of the actions of the foot which produce the sounds have been given distinguishing names; these terms constitute an oral and written vocabulary. The difficulty lies in the fact that there is some diversity of terminology. Efforts have been made to standardize terminology but universality has not yet been achieved. Books in which dances are recorded contain glossaries or sections devoted to the terminology used by the author. In each case, the terminology must be committed to memory before the recorded dances can be put into action.

The best place to start is with the simplest actions of the foot which produce *one* sound. These constitute the *Basic Movements* which are combined into a great variety of patterns to form a distinct *Sequence* of movement which may be repeated to form a *Part* or section of a dance, usually an eight-measure phrase of music. The Sequence may be one measure long, two measures, three measures, possibly four measures; if it is short (one or two measures) and is repeated during the eight-measure duration, it becomes monotonous so a contrast in movement and sound is desirable. A change in pattern, a different Sequence, is added to complete the Part. This is called a *Break*. It means just that—a break or change in the flow of sound for the purpose of interest and contrast. The Parts of a dance are related to the phrases of the music which has been chosen for accompaniment. A simple dance using a chorus of popular music will have four Parts—four phrases of eight measures. The number of measures for the Sequence, the repetitions, and the Break will total eight measures. The arrangement or order of the Sequence and Break within the eight measures need not follow just one structural progression.

## BASIC MOVEMENTS—ONE SOUND

*Step.* One sound actions are the basic movements: these provide the backbone, the major body of material. The first to try is a *Step*— a walking step. The action is changed slightly from the normal walking step. Instead of contacting the floor with the heel first, carry the weight a little forward and contact the floor with the toe of the shoe, the sole of the foot immediately following. Even when moving backward or sideward, the weight line falls through the ball of the foot. With each step, there is a change of body weight from one foot to the other. Stand with your weight on the left foot. STEP R—transfer the weight to the right foot as you move forward. Practice walking in different directions until you get clear sharp sounds. In almost all movement patterns in tap, the weight is carried over the ball of the foot.

*Run.* Increase the size or the speed of the walk so that the body is lifted for a second into the air. This is a run—one clear, sharp sound as the toe strikes the floor each time a transfer of weight is made from one foot to the other.

*Hop.* Stand with the weight on one foot; push the body into the air and with no transfer of weight, land on the *same* foot.

*Leap.* Stand with the weight on one foot; push the body into the air and land on the *other* foot. Done continuously the leap is like a run, only a little higher or longer.

*Jump.* Stand with the weight on both feet; push the body into the air and land on *both* feet. This should produce one sound. If on landing, one foot contacts the floor slightly before the other, you will hear two sounds. You may also stand on both feet, go into the air, and land on one foot, or start with the weight on one foot, go into the air, and land on both feet. Each produces the one sound but the action is a little different.

*Brush.* Stand with the weight on one foot. Swing the other leg freely forward, backward, and from side to side. The movement stems from the hip joint; there is little knee action. At the lowest point in the arc, the toe strikes the floor and produces one sound. The size of this basic movement is rather large; the direction may be forward, backward, to the left or to the right side. If the direction is not designated, the action is forward. BRUSH R to L would be interpreted as brushing the right leg across to the left. BRUSH R would mean to brush the right leg forward. The brushing action normally refers to the contact of the toe with the floor. With a sharply flexed ankle, however, the heel may contact the floor at the lowest point of the arc. If this is desired, add the qualifying description—HEEL BRUSH.

*Front—Back.* Practice the leg swings slowly and feel the full extent of the movement. Begin to make the swinging arc smaller and faster as the foot moves forward and back. As the size is reduced and the speed increased, the arc is decreased, the hip joint action is slight, and the flexion and extension of the knee and ankle becomes greater. This small short action of the foot moving forward making one sound is called a FRONT; the backward movement making one sound is called a BACK. Stand with the weight on the left foot, the right foot slightly lifted off the floor but next to the left foot. Briskly move the right toe forward or back making one clear sound. Stand with both feet on the floor but with the weight on the left foot; briskly move the right toe backward making one clear sound. This Basic Movement backward from the foot on the floor position is sometimes called a "pick-up"—you have to pick up the toe slightly before the sound can be made as the foot moves backward. With the *Brush, Front,* and *Back* there is no transfer of weight from one foot to the other. At the end of the action, the foot is in the air.

*Toe Tap.* Stand with the weight on one foot and lightly touch the toe tap or the toe of the other foot on the floor—in front of, to either side, or in back of the supporting foot. Indicate the spot with an appropriate word. No weight change is made. TOE TAP R behind L would mean to touch the right toe behind the left foot.

*Toe Snap.* With the weight on one foot, place the heel of the other foot on the floor with the toe lifted off the floor. Snap the toe to the

**What is the difference between a step and a flap? a front and a brush?**

Evaluation Questions

floor making one sound as you transfer the weight to that foot. If by any chance you do not want a weight transfer, indicate this in the description. TOE SNAP R no weight means to snap the right toe to the floor but keep the weight on the left foot.

*Stamp.* This signifies what the word customarily means. The whole foot is placed firmly and sharply on the floor. This is another of the Basic Movements which may or may not be done with a transfer of weight. Normally there is a transfer of weight. If you want the stamping foot to be released so it can move immediately, simply write STAMP R—no weight.

*Chug—Pull.* With the weight on one foot, slide forward on the foot, making a scuffing sound. This is a *Chug*. When the direction is backward, call it a *Pull*. These sounds are not clear and sharp and there is no change of weight. Like the *Front* and *Back*, these terms indicate specific direction in movement.

*Heel Drop.* Now for the heel actions. Stand with the weight on the ball of the foot. Drop the heel to the floor making a clear sharp sound. There is no change of weight.

*Heel.* Step forward, in place, or sideward on the heel with the toe lifted. There is a change of weight and a sound that is clear but not as sharp as in the *Heel Drop*. If you simply want to touch the heel to the floor and not transfer the weight, write HEEL R—no weight.

With these 15 one-sound actions, an infinite variety of patterns can be formed. As patterns and terminology have developed, however, a few two- and three-sound actions have become such a standard part of tap material that they should be mentioned.

Evaluation Questions

In which direction do you move with a drawback? a chug? a pull?

## BASIC MOVEMENTS—TWO SOUNDS

*Ball-Change.* This is a *Step-Step*. The action is uneven rhythmically; the first *Step* is quicker than the second *Step*. Since both feet are involved, the sequence of foot action must be recorded. BALL-CHANGE L-R means to stand with the weight on the R foot, step on the L toe, and quickly back to the R foot.

*Shuffle.* This is a *Front* and a *Back,* the small forward and backward action of the foot. There is no change of weight; the moving foot is left in the air. Usually it is done moving directly forward and back but it can be done to the side. SHUFFLE R to R indicates that you would shuffle the right toe to the right side. This action is sometimes called a "double" or a "two."

*Flap—Drawback.* These terms, like the *Chug* and *Pull, Front* and *Back,* indicate the direction of the action. They are directly related to the *Step* or normal walking action. As the leading foot moves forward for the transfer of weight, let the toe tap strike the floor just before the weight is transferred for the *Step*. Make two clear sounds. The toe does not swing forward as in a *Front* and then *Step*, but rather the extra sound is dropped in just before the stepping action is completed. Practice it slowly walking forward. As control of the toe is mastered, increase the speed. Then try doing it in place and moving sideward. The *Drawback* is the *Flap* moving backward with the extra sound dropped in just before the transfer of weight. Stand with the feet together but with the weight on the right foot; flex the left ankle keeping the heel on the floor with the toe raised. Move the left foot back letting the toe tap brush the floor and then step on the left foot, producing two clear sounds. Start with long slow steps moving backward. Then increase the speed

**19**

Which basic movement would you choose to move through each spatial design?

Evaluation Questions

SPATIAL DESIGN

and shorten the length of each step. In performing both the *Flap* and the *Drawback*, be sure that both sounds are clear.

## BASIC MOVEMENTS—THREE SOUNDS

*Triple.* The *Triple* adds a *Step* to the *Shuffle*: *Front, Back, Step,* thus making three sounds with a change of weight. This action is sometimes called a "three."

There are other combinations of Basic Movements that are so frequently used that they too have been given names which are generally understood by all tap dancers. A few of these will be found in the Appendix—*Waltz Step, Buffalo, Irish Step, Time Step*. These are commonly called "steps" but this terminology leads to a double meaning for that word. In relation to the terminology developed in this chapter, they are combinations of Basic Movements which could be used as a Sequence or a Break. The word "step" is sometimes also used to designate a section of a dance; in this chapter, however, the word Part is employed. Confusion results when there are double or triple meanings for one word.

Your Basic Movement vocabulary is now complete, as well as the terms used to describe the building blocks of a dance: *Sequence, Break, Parts*. When the dance is recorded, the Parts are numbered with Roman numerals such as I, II, III, IV. Within each Part the Sequences are identified in order with the letters A, B, C, and the like. The Sequences are described with their rhythmic count, action vocabulary, appropriate foot, and direction of movement. If a Sequence is repeated in a later Part, this can be indicated by number and letter; e.g., counts 1-3, 1-3 Repeat I A. A diagram of the floor pattern helps to clarify the spatial design.

Diagram A:

SPATIAL DESIGN

One more thing must be said. The terminology for the Basic Movements refers only to the foot action. It would be very misleading to leave you with the impression that a dancer's only concern is with the action of the body from the waist down. True, the focal point of tap is on the sound patterns produced by the foot action, but the whole person dances and the actions of the whole body are important to the total design of the dance. Actions other than foot actions must be fully described. These actions are not usually given in a tap dance recording. They become a part of the individual's interpretation of the dance; this is a personal or group invention in order to add interest and to project a style or a characterization. Actions are usually exaggerated either by overstatement or understatement for emphasis. The important thing is that the whole body should be active with patterns complementary to the foot action. There should be a total flow of good movement. Good movement is vigorous, natural, vital, and in keeping with the idea projected and the sophistication of the group dancing. Freedom from excess tensions in any one part of the body and good balance are extremely important. As the feet move quickly making rapid changes of weight from one foot to the other, the torso, head, and arms may counterbalance the foot and leg movements. The dancer who has good control of his body and who moves freely usually will also have greater rhythmic accuracy and will produce a clearer sound pattern.

## ACTION PROBLEMS

Can you put these Basic Movements into a Sequence?

1. Step L, Heel Drop L, Step R, Heel Drop R, Step L, Step R, Step L, Heel Drop L.
2. Drawback L, Flap R to R, Flap L over R, Brush R, Heel Drop L.
3. Triple L, Triple R, Triple L, Step R, Step L.

**21**

# 6

# What Is the Beat?
# —Time Analysis

It is not enough to make interesting sound patterns with the feet. These sound patterns must relate harmoniously and accurately with the musical accompaniment. You need, therefore, to recognize meters, measures, and phrases, and half, quarter, and eighth notes and to identify relationships.

Most tap dances use a 4/4 or a 3/4 meter, jazz or waltz music. The 4/4 meter has four quarter notes, or the counting equivalent, in each measure; a strong accent occurs on count 1 and a lesser accent on count 3. The 3/4 meter has three quarter notes, or their equivalent, in each measure with a strong accent on count 1. The duration of time for the note is the smallest time division; the notes are then grouped in measures, the measures into phrases, and the phrases into a composition. It is particularly important to be able to recognize the relationships between whole, half, quarter, and eighth notes and to be able to write and verbalize the count. In most music, the following note-count combination is applicable:

|  | whole | half | quarter | eighth | sixteenth |
|---|---|---|---|---|---|
| NOTE | ○ | ♩ ♩ | ♩♩♩♩ | ♫ ♫ ♫ ♫ | ♬ ♬ ♬ ♬ |
| COUNT | 1(234) | 1(2)3(4) | 1234 | 1&2&3&4& | 1a&a2a&a3a&a4a&a |

In most popular music, the chorus is thirty-two measures and is divided into four phrases of eight measures each. The feeling of rest or pause at the end of a phrase is the signal to conclude one Part and to begin a new Part at the beginning of the new phrase.

Tempo refers to rate of speed; it indicates the fastness or slowness of the flow of the quarter-note pulse. Moderate tempo is good for the beginning tap dancer. A fast tempo may be used when skill has been acquired. Certain types of dances have characteristic speeds. A Soft Shoe is usually lazy and slow while a Jig is brittle and fast. Character dances or impersonations use speeds which are appropriate to the idea. It is important for the dancer to establish the tempo of the music and then to be able to hold that pulse (speed) constant when practicing without the music. If you count quickly when the pattern of movement is easy and then slow your count during the more difficult Sequences, the result will be a distorted, uneven tempo. You must keep an even, regular count, the same duration for each quarter note or one count and for each measure. You may count slowly for a Sequence and Break as long as this is kept in correct proportion; as the Part is perfected, increase the speed until the desired tempo is reached.

If all sounds are made on the quarter note or on the eighth note, the resulting rhythmic patterns will be dull. Diversity in sound pattern, the rhythmic pattern, is important in order to maintain interest. Accenting or emphasizing beats other than the major musical accents is a device which adds interest. Snycopation results when the movement accents are placed on the weak beats or normally unaccented beats in a measure.

One last word on Time patterns. Many movement Sequences begin with an "up beat" in tap dance. This is a lift in movement, a lightness in sound, which occurs before the accent of the first musical count. When the movement and sound start *before* count 1, an additional emphasis is given to count 1 with the lift and fall of the body. An example in count would be 4&1; in notation it would be ♫|♩̂ . The sound pattern rides over the bar line and gives a different flavor to the Sequence. If the pattern of movement and sound starts on count 1, the Sequence begins with a "down beat." Do 2 Triples in 4/4, counting it 4& 1 2& 3; this uses the "up beat." Then do the 2 Triples, counting it 1& 2 3& 4. Listen for the difference in sound; there is also a difference in the feel of the action.

## ACTION PROBLEMS

Can you do a STEP R, BALL-CHANGE L-R, and repeat to the L?

> 4/4 Jazz    a.   1 & 2 3 & 4
>             b.   4 & 1 2 & 3

At the end of the section on Basic Movements (p. 21), there are three Sequences described. Take the first Sequence, no. 1. Choose a moderate tempo 4/4 jazz record; change the STEP to a FLAP; add a variation, and do the whole to the following rhythmic pattern. This is the first Part of your tap dance. The movements are planned to fit the counts indicated in the columns. The first Sequence is lettered A, the second is B, and the Break is C.

## TIME ANALYSIS

|  |  | COUNT | DESCRIPTION |
|---|---|---|---|
| PART I. | A. | a 1 | Flap L |
|  |  | 2 | Heel Drop L |
|  |  | a 3 | Flap R |
|  |  | 4 | Heel Drop R |
|  |  | a 1 | Flap L |
|  |  | a 2 | Flap R |
|  |  | a 3 | Flap L |
|  |  | 4 | Heel Drop L |
|  |  | a 1-4) | Repeat A |
|  |  |  | starting R |
|  |  | a 1-4) |  |

(VARIATION ON A)

|  | COUNT | DESCRIPTION |
|---|---|---|
| B. | a 1 | Flap L |
|  | a 2 | Flap R |
|  | a 3 | Flap L |
|  | 4 | Heel Drop L |
|  | a 1 | Flap R |
|  | a 2 | Flap L |
|  | a 3 | Flap R |
|  | 4 | Heel Drop R |

You now have: A consisting of 2 measures; a repetition for 2 measures; a variation which is B for 2 measures. A change in sound and movement is needed for contrast—a Break—to complete the 8-measure phrase.

|  | COUNT | DESCRIPTION |
|---|---|---|
| C. | 1 | Jump forward |
|  | 2 | Snap fingers |
| Break | 3 | Jump backward |
|  | 4 | Snap fingers |
|  | (1) | Hold |
|  | a 2 | Flap L |
|  | a 3 | Flap R |
|  | (4) | Hold |

This is Part I of your first 4/4 Rhythm Routine—8 measures.

# Where Are You Going?
# —Space Analysis

While the movement and sound patterns are being determined, thought should be given to the *area* in which the dance is to be performed and to the location of the audience. The area is three-dimensional; it has height and width and depth. If the area is small, the dancer must not look crowded; if the area is large, the dancer should not cling to the center and look lonely. The dance should be planned to fill the space. This does not mean that the dancer continuously roves around and about so that all parts of the area are used at one time or another. It does mean that the total area is planned for use in the best possible way in relation to the purpose of the dance.

When the usual proscenium stage is used, the dance is framed with the arch in front, side curtains or wings, and a back curtain. The audience looks at a moving design from one angle. If a circular stage is used, there is no picture frame and the audience is dispersed all around the dance area. The dancer must consciously plan the designs in the space that the audience will see. All that the modern dance or ballet has discovered about the use of the stage space is not only available to the tap dancer but is also pertinent to his planning of spatial design. A common misconception is the belief that the dancer should always face the audience. This may be a carry-over from the time long ago when the tap dancer performed between the front stage curtain and the footlights as an interlude between acts of a performance. The lack of performing depth produced a kind of two-dimensional design. The *directional* paths of forward, backward, sideward to right or left, up and down produce different designs when the facing of the dancer is changed. The directional path is established in relation to the front of the dancer. Variety is added in the repetition of a Sequence simply by

Place facing symbols ♂ on this floor pattern to indicate where the dancer could move forward, backward, sideward L, sideward R.

Evaluation Questions

FLOOR PATTERN

changing the dancer's relationship to the frame of the stage. Remember, too, that the directional path may follow a straight line or a curved line.

Although most of the actual sound-producing movements of the feet are small in size, or *dimension,* the dancer must give attention to the total action of the body. Large actions oppose small actions. The total shape of the movement Sequences and Breaks should include contrasting dimensions. Holding the arms out to the side throughout the entire dance inhibits free use of the body and leads to monotony.

The direction of the gaze, the *focus,* of the dancer contributes to purposeful performance, the dramatic intent, and the style of the dancer. The audience is very much aware of where the dancer is looking. Mood, character identification, dramatic incident are enhanced by careful planning of focus.

One aspect of spatial planning which is used effectively by other forms of dance but which has been neglected by the tap dancer is the use of different *levels* for body placement. Tappers have used stairs, steps, ramps, and platforms for moving up and down and around to enhance design. They use jumps and leaps to project the body into the air; but they rarely use the floor for a low-level body position. Since the sound making is done with the taps on the floor, the low-level body placement does present problems, but there are possibilities here for the inventive mind.

The spatial design that the dance makes is the result of the action patterns, the directional path, the dimensions of movement, the focus of the dancer, the level of the body placement, all in relation to the space available. This spatial design may be symmetrical or asymmetrical. The symmetrical tends to the static, the asymmetrical to the dynamic. Dance should be exciting, stimulating, vital; the use of asymmetrical

Diagram B:

FLOOR PATTERN

designs helps to produce this effect. The actions of the body—what the feet and legs, torso and arms are doing—may be symmetrical or asymmetrical. If you continuously do something to the left, and then to the right, or forward and then backward, this produces a static quality. The floor pattern, the sequence of directional paths, may be symmetrical or asymmetrical. Draw the design that the directional paths produce. This makes you aware of the two-dimensional spatial design.

All these aspects of spatial planning—the area, directions of movement and the facing of the dancer, dimensions of movement, focus, level, the symmetrical and asymmetrical design—are basic to the planning of a dance whether it is for one person or for ten. With a group, there are simply more people to plan for and there are greater possibilities for complexity in interest and design. The interaction between dancers and the area builds excitement. A well-planned group dance for five people *needs* five people. It is not merely a dance for one person but must be danced by five. In other words, the design depends on the number of people planned for and is not as effective with fewer dancers or more dancers. A very simple group dance may be quite effective if the dancers are so arranged that facings and directional paths develop oppositional patterns even though the dancers are all doing the same thing at the same time—*unison* movement. Placing dancers in an asymmetrical grouping strengthens the oppositional relationships. Figure 1 shows a floor pattern for one dancer facing the audience. Contrast it with Figure 2. Three dancers, two against one, do exactly the same thing but start from opposite corners and move toward each other. One slight modification could be to have the three dancers end facing the audience.

Breaking the group into sub-groups provides more complexity not only in spatial design but also in rhythmic design. Group may move

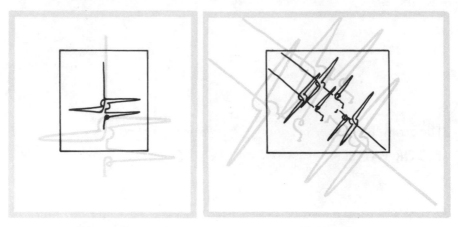

Figure 1                              Figure 2

against group at the same time with different but related patterns, *counterpoint;* one person may move and the others answer, with the same or a related pattern, *responsorial;* group may answer group with the same or a related pattern, *antiphonal;* or, with the same or a related pattern, each person in the group may move quickly one after the other, a kind of follow the leader, in *succession.* All these devices build group interaction, add interest, and enhance design.

## ACTION PROBLEMS

Can you do?                              in place?

| Count | Description | |
|---|---|---|
| a 1 | Flap L | |
| a 2 | Ball-Change R-L | moving from side to side? |
| a 3 | Flap R | |
| a 4 | Ball-Change L-R | |
| a 1 | Flap L | in place during measure 1 and |
| a 2 | Flap R | a complete turn during meas- |
| a 3 | Flap L | ure 2? |
| a 4 | Ball-Change R-L | |

Go back to the end of the section on Basic Movements (p. 21). Practice 2. Do it to this count and add a Break.

This is the second Part of your first tap dance. (Part I is at the end of the section on Time Analysis, p. 24.) So far, the floor pattern is quite symmetrical.

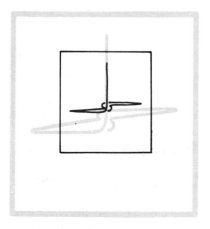

*Figure 3*

| COUNT | DESCRIPTION | | COUNT | DESCRIPTION |
|---|---|---|---|---|
| PART II. A. a 1 | Drawback L behind R | | B. a 1 | Drawback L |
| | | | 2 | Heel Drop L |
| a 2 | Flap R to R | Break | a 3 | Drawback R |
| a 3 | Flap L over R | | 4 | Heel Drop R |
| & | Brush R | | 1 | Cross L over R |
| 4 | Heel Drop L | | (2) | Hold |
| a 1-4 | Repeat A to L | | 3 | Pivot 1/2 turn to R |
| | | | (4) | Hold |

C. 4 measures. Repeat *A* and *B*

# 8

# What Do You Have to Say? —Content and Style

Tap, just as other forms of dance, may communicate an idea, a feeling, a story, or it may only intend to present a moving temporal design in space. If it intends to communicate, it is *Dramatic* with the emphasis on the idea, character impersonation, mood or feeling, or narrative. Although the choice of pattern is determined by the dramatic content, this does not deemphasize the sound patterns. The spatial design and the choice of music are also influenced by the content. The possibilities for dramatic content are almost limitless.

If there is no dramatic intent, no plan to communicate idea or impersonation, the dance is *Abstract;* the entire interest lies in the movement, temporal, and spatial designs. There is great variety here. The Waltz can range from the simple, slow, large movement "clogs" to the very intricate and fast 3/4 rhythm waltzes. The 4/4 routines can range from the simple to the highly complex, from the slow and languid to the brittle and fast tempos. Besides the 4/4 regular jazz, there are two other popular styles in 4/4, the Soft Shoe and the Military. The Soft Shoe, first done without taps on the shoes so that a soft, slurring sound was made, tends to the slower more languid tempos. The body is used with great flexibility and with large swinging motions. The Military is more rigid, more vertical, with drum sounds made by the feet. Then there is the Jig, the 6/8 meter, with fast Triples on the eighth notes. These last three, the Soft Shoe, Military, and Jig, border on the character dances or impersonations. The dividing line can be so thin that it is barely discernible.

In both the Dramatic and Abstract dance, there should be a consideration of *style*. In the Abstract dance it is the projection of self, the personal style of moving developed by the dancer. Three solo dancers may do exactly the same dance but the audience will respond a little differently to each because of the personal, individual manner of projection of self. Confidence, ease, and assurance must radiate from the dancer. At no moment should the audience feel any tension, any worry for a possible loss of balance or forgetfulness. If the dance is Dramatic, the style is closely related to content. The dividing line may be hazy. If communication of mood or feeling is the dancer's intent, the style will probably be personal; if it is impersonation or narrative, the style will conform to characterization.

A dance might be Abstract and yet borrow a period style. A dance might be planned in Folk style or Court style. The distinction between the two types of dances could be hazy. The style is definite; but are you dancing in the style of the Minuet, or are you impersonating the lady of fashion dancing a Minuet? It really is not necessary to labor the point.

One further word on style. Men and women dance with a different manner. They do, and they should. With equal abilities, each can perform the same patterns, but the manner or style of performance will be different. With a mixed group the contrast in styles should be exploited so that each enhances the other.

*Figure 4*

**31**

## ACTION PROBLEMS

Do the Sequence at the left in the suggested tempos.

4/4 meter

| Count | Description | |
|---|---|---|
| 4 & 1 | Triple L | Slow 4/4; be a scarecrow |
| 2 & 3 | Triple R | Fast 4/4; be a puppet on a string |
| 4 & 1 | Triple L | March 4/4; be a soldier |
| 2 | Step R | Moderate 4/4; sneak up on some- |
| 3 | Step L | one intending to surprise |

3/4 meter

| Count | Description | |
|---|---|---|
| 2 3 1 | Triple L | Slow 3/4; be an ice skater |
| 2 3 1 | Triple R | Fast 3/4; sharp clear sounds; be |
| 2 3 1 | Triple L | yourself |
| (2) | Hold | |
| 3 | Step R | |
| 1 | Step L | |

6/8 meter

| Count | Description | |
|---|---|---|
| 5 6 1 | Triple L | Fast 6/8; with body very con- |
| 2 3 4 | Triple R | trolled and vertical, be an Irish |
| 5 6 1 | Triple L | Folk Dancer |
| (2) | Hold | |
| 3 | Step R | |
| 4 | Step L | |

This Part will be based on 3 A at the end of the section on Basic Movements (p. 21). This is the third Part of your tap dance.

| | Count | Description | | Count | Description |
|---|---|---|---|---|---|
| Part III. A. | 4 & 1 | Triple L | B. | 4 & 1 | Triple L |
| | 2 & 3 | Triple R | | 2 | Step R |
| | 4 & 1 | Triple L | | 3 | Step L |
| | 2 | Step R | | 4 & 1–3 | Repeat *B* |
| | 3 | Step L | | | starting R |
| | 4 & 1–3 | Repeat *A* | | | |
| | | starting R | | | |

C. 1-4)  Repeat  Break I *C* (p. 24)
   1-4)

# How Do You
# Put it Together?
# —Structure

Let's go back and review. The Basic Movements are the simple one, two, three sound patterns. These are combined in a particular way to form a short Sequence. The Sequence may be repeated exactly or it may be varied. A new Sequence may be added to change the sound pattern. If you have completed eight measures, the Sequence used as the phrase ending is called a Break. The Sequences and the Break make up one Part. A normal thirty-two measure chorus is divided into four phrases. Note that you will have four Parts in a short thirty-two measure dance. The Parts may be built in many different ways. As an illustration, let each Sequence be two measures long. The following are some of the Sequence combinations possible: A A B B, A B A B, A A B C, A B B C, A B C D.

If you are using the standard chorus, you can actually build your dance without music, but it is much more fun to work with a particular piece of music. Sometimes the rhythmic patterns and the melody inspire sound and movement patterns. Some popular pieces of music do not follow the standard four phrases of eight measures; after the music is selected, you must listen carefully to identify the phrases so that the dance and music are built in the same way. Of course, if your dance is to be Dramatic, the choice of music must be compatible with the content or purpose of the dance. If it is an Abstract dance, you look for pleasing melody, good orchestration, and steady tempo. When you are working with music other than the popular chorus, the structure of the dance should follow the musical form. The simple one-, two-, and three-part sequential forms are quite adaptable. These are often abbreviated as A, A B, A B A, A B C; here the letters refer to the parts of the musical form and not to the Sequence movement. There is no reason why the Theme and Variation, Rondo, or Ground Bass could not be used; and a Round in tap is great fun. Actually the standard chorus, if you think of the phrases as musical parts, has an A A B A form. The first, second, and fourth phrases have the same melody but the third phrase is different.

However you develop your dance, keep in mind the aesthetic principles of *Unity, Variety, Repetition, Contrast,* and *Transition.* All parts should be related and significant to the idea; a Sequence may be varied by changing the direction, dimension, level, focus, or by using the same Basic Movements in a little different combination; Breaks or Sequences may be repeated; new material, different Sequences, are needed for contrast. Not only the Sequences but also the Parts must join together logically. You cannot start Part II on the right foot if the weight is on the right foot at the end of Part I. If there is an easy flow of movement from the beginning to end, the other principles of balance, sequence, proportion, and climax will fall into line and the dance will have a feeling of harmony.

## ACTION PROBLEM

Now to get back to the dance. You have completed Parts I, II, III or 24 measures (see p. 24, 29, 32). Part IV will tie the whole together. This is the last Part of your first tap dance.

PART IV. COUNT    DESCRIPTION

| | | |
|---|---|---|
| A. | a 1-4) | Repeat I A (p. 24) |
| | a 1-4) | |
| B. | a 1-4) | Repeat II A starting on the R and moving to the L (p. 29) |
| | a 1-4) | |
| C. | a 1-4) | Repeat II B making a full turn (p. 29) |
| | a 1-4) | |
| D. | 1 | Jump forward |
| Final | 2 | Snap fingers |
| Break | 3 | Jump backward |
| | 4 | Snap fingers |
| | 1 | Step L |
| | 2 | Brush R |
| | 3 | Chug   L |
| | (4) | Hold |

The spatial design has now changed from symmetrical at the end of Part III to asymmetrical. To illustrate the aesthetic principles, Part I is based on the Flap and Heel Drop; Sequence A is repeated; B is a variation of A; C is the contrasting material and is used as the Break.

Evaluation Questions

In the finished dance, which sequences are symmetrical? asymmetrical? Which directions are used? Which sequences start with an up beat? a down beat?

Part II adds the Brush and a change in direction; Sequences A and B are repeated. Part III adds contrasting new material—the Triple; Sequence A is repeated; B is a variation of A; the Break of Part I is repeated at the end of Part III. Part IV repeats Part I *A*, Part II *A* and *B* with a full turn, and completes with a change in the ending of the break used in Parts I and III. There are illustrations here of *Unity*—all sequences seem to belong together; *Variety, Repetition, Contrast,* and smooth *Transitions.* Is there a feeling of *Harmony?*

This is a "beginning" dance. It can be done alone, or it could be done with a group. To make it more interesting as a group dance, try incorporating some of the group devices mentioned in the chapter on spatial design. With an understanding of compositional principles and skill in the performance of the Basic Movements, you are ready to make up your own dance. (For the description of a "beginning" waltz dance, refer to the Appendix.)

*How do you start?* First decide what kind of dance you want to do. Choose your music; listen carefully for phrasing. Then begin to "play" with the Basic Movements. Improvise until you have something that sounds and feels pleasing. This will be your first Sequence. Repeat it or vary it or add something new to complete the phrase. Part I is finished. When it feels right and you like it, stop and analyze what you have done. Then go on to the next Part. When the whole dance is finished, check the floor pattern and the aesthetic principles. When you have ironed out any problem spots, write it down. The complexity of your dances will increase as your skill increases. Do not forget to analyze what you have done as soon as you are satisfied with a Part.

*How do you know if it is a "good" dance?* You have the answer to this question if you have carefully analyzed each Part as you were build-

**In the spaces in the box, write the names of the Basic Movements used in the completed dance and the number of sounds in each. Check where there is a change of weight.**

Evaluation Questions

BASIC
MOVEMENTS

ing the dance. The following questions will help you evaluate your own original dances. They may also be used as criteria for evaluating the dances composed by other people.

Is the sound interesting? (temporal analysis)
> Are the sound patterns sufficiently varied?
> Does the movement phrase begin and end with the music phrase?
> Does the speed of the movement pattern suit the tempo of the music?

Is the spatial design interesting? (spatial analysis)
> Are several directions used?
> Are different facing used?
> Is the floor pattern interesting?
> Does the floor pattern adequately relate to the dance space?
> Is the focus clearly established?
> If it is a group dance, do the dancers relate to each other? to the audience?

What is the purpose of the dance? (content and style)
> Is it an abstract dance?
> Is the style appropriate?
> Is the choice of meter and tune appealing?
> Are the movement, temporal, and spatial designs sufficiently dynamic?
> Is it a Dramatic Dance?
> Is the idea danceable?
> Does the dance add something new or fresh to the idea?
> Is the style appropriate?
> Is the choice of music appropriate?

Diagram C:

BASIC
MOVEMENTS

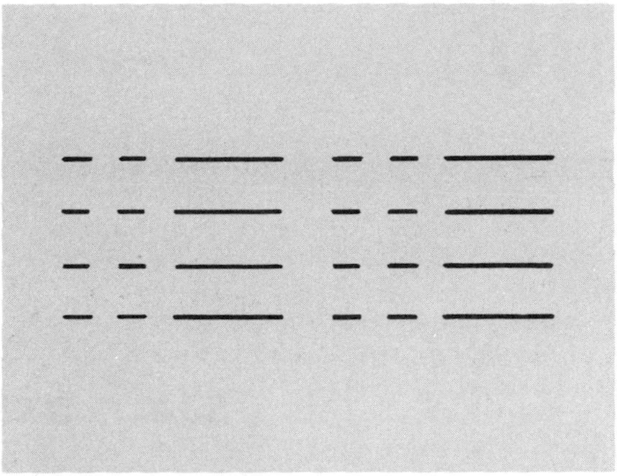

How is the dance structured?
    Are the Sequences, Breaks, Parts put together logically?
    Does the dance hang together? Does it have a feeling of unity?
    Are the transitions logical?
    Is there variety, contrast, and some repetition?
    Does the dance "feel" good?

How well is the dance performed?
    Are the sounds sharp and clear?
    Does the body move easily and freely?
    Is there variation in the body action?
    Is the dance performed with confidence?

# 10

# Dance Problems

It is relatively easy to learn a dance which someone else has composed. To be told what to do and when to do it taxes the imitative powers but does not stimulate personal inventiveness. Tap can only be a creative experience when you use material in your own way. The possibilities are so unlimited that the problem becomes not what to do but where to start. Since a tap dance at this elementary level can be broken into small pieces (Sequences), it has an advantage over other creative dance efforts. Each small piece can be joined to another small piece to form larger and larger compositions. If you can do each piece starting with either the right or left foot, even the transitions present no problems.

To help you get started, three sets of problems are presented. The first, a 3/4 waltz, is an approach through movement and rhythmic Sequences; it suggests structure, floor pattern, and style. The second problem, a 4/4 jazz, is an approach through Sequences built on directional paths; it suggests structure, floor pattern, and style. The third problem suggests ideas for content.

Start where you wish—but start. The fun in solving a problem comes only by doing. The skill of performance comes only by doing. The pride in creation comes only by doing.

I. A. *Movement and rhythmic patterns.* Choose a 3/4 waltz with moderate tempo. Do not use the waltz step.

1. Make a 2-measure Sequence with: Step, Toe Tap, Chug, Brush.
2. Make a 3-measure Sequence with: Heel, Hop, Toe Snap, Shuffle, Stamp.
3. Make a 4-measure Sequence with: Triple, Heel Drop, Ball-Change, Flap.

4. Make a Sequence to the count of: 1 & 2 & 3, 1(2) 3.
5. Make a Sequence to the count of: & 1 2 3,  1 2 (3).

Can you do each Sequence starting with the R foot? L foot? Do some of the Sequences have a directional path?

B.  *Structure*: 32 measures. Consider the Sequences developed in 1 A as Breaks. Combine these with the waltz step. (For a description of the waltz step see Appendix A p. 43.) Be sure that as you put the Sequences together the transitions are smooth.

This structural pattern for the dance is fairly easy.

|  |  | MEASURES | SEQUENCE |
|---|---|---|---|
| PART I. | A. | 2 measures—2 waltz steps | |
| | B. | 2 measures developed as #1 | |
| | C. | 2 measures—2 waltz steps | |
| | D. | 2 measures developed as #4 | |
| II. | A. | 2 measures—2 waltz steps | |
| | B. | 3 measures developed as #2 | |
| | C. | 3 measures—repeat II *B* | |
| III. | A. | 4 measures developed as #3 | |
| | B. | 2 measures—2 waltz steps | |
| | C. | 2 measures—repeat I *D* | |
| IV. | A. | 2 measures—2 waltz steps | |
| | B. | 2 measures developed as #5 | |
| | C. | 2 measures—2 waltz steps | |
| | D. | 2 measures—repeat I *D* | |

This structural pattern for the dance is more difficult.

|  |  | MEASURES | SEQUENCE |
|---|---|---|---|
| PART I. | A. | 1 measure—1 waltz step | |
| | B. | 2 measures developed as #1 | |
| | C. | 1 measure—1 waltz step | |
| | D. | 2 measures—repeat I *B* | |
| | E. | 2 measures developed as #4 | |
| II. | A. | 3 measures developed as #2 | |
| | B. | 1 measure—1 waltz step | |
| | C. | 2 measures—repeat I *B* | |
| | D. | 2 measures—repeat I *D* | |
| III. | A. | 2 measures—2 waltz steps | |
| | B. | 4 measures developed as #3 | |
| | C. | 2 measures—repeat I *D* | |

IV.  A.  2 measures developed as #5
    B.  3 measures—repeat II *A*
    C.  1 measure—1 waltz step
    D.  2 measures—repeat I *D*

C.  *Floor pattern*
1. Draw the floor pattern.

2. Change the floor pattern by extending, or contracting, or changing the directional path.

3. Place the floor pattern of #2 in a different relationship to the dance space.

D.  *Style.* Add appropriate body actions to the dance so that you dance as:
1. A Raggedy Ann.
2. A puppet on strings.

II.  A.  *Spatial patterns*—directional paths. Choose a 4/4 jazz with moderate tempo.
1. Make a 4 measure Sequence that moves forward.
2. Make a 2 measure Sequence that involves a full turn in place.
3. Make a 6 measure Sequence that moves in an arc with 3 complete turns.
4. Make a 2 measure Sequence that moves backward on the R diagonal and repeats on the L diagonal.
5. Make a 2 measure Sequence that moves sideward L.

Can you do each sequence starting with the R foot? L foot?
Can you do each sequence in the opposite direction?

B.  *Structure*: 32 measures. Be sure that, as you put the Sequences together, the transitions are smooth.

| | | MEASURES | SEQUENCE |
|---|---|---|---|
| PART I. | A. | 4 measures developed as #1 | |
| | B. | 2 measures developed as #2 | |
| | C. | 2 measures—repeat I *B* without turning | |
| II. | A. | 6 measures developed as #3 | |
| | B. | 2 measures—repeat I *C* | |

III.  A.  4 measures developed as #4
    B.  2 measures—repeat measures 1 and 2 of III *A*
    C.  2 measures—repeat I *C*

IV.  A.  2 measures developed as #5
       2 measures—repeat IV *A*
    B.  2 measures—repeat measures 1 and 2 of I *A*
    C.  2 measures—repeat I *B* to end facing audience

C.  *Floor pattern.* This symbol ♂ indicates the body facing.
    1.  Moving directly forward toward the audience, the floor pattern would look like this. Figure 5
    2.  Try it like this. Figure 6
    3.  Try it like this. Figure 7

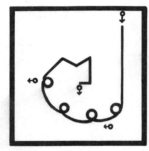 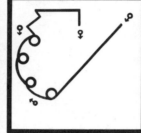 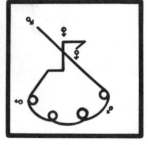

    *Figure 5*        *Figure 6*        *Figure 7*

D.  *Style.* Add appropriate body actions to the dance so that you dance as:
    1.  A slinky siren with a scarf.
    2.  A waitress with an imaginary tray.
    3.  A student with an armload of books.

III.  *Content.* The following ideas will suggest content and style:
    A.  3/4 waltz: 32 measures. Dance as:
        1.  A child playing hopscotch and jumping rope.
        2.  A window shopper before Christmas.

    B.  4/4 Jazz: 32 measures. Dance as if you are:
        1.  Arriving at an airport just prior to flight time.
        2.  Young lady with an umbrella. Use the umbrella as a sound-producing agent.

C. Nursery rhymes
1. Establish the rhythmic pattern of the words in the sound pattern of dance.
2. Add appropriate body action to the dance to identify the rhyme.

D. Rounds: "Row, row, row your boat," "Down at the station," or any other favorite.

Use the ideas suggested in the words of the Round as the stimulus for developing the movement and rhythmic patterns. Be sure to add appropriate body actions.

1. Plan the dance for one dancer.
2. Arrange the dance for five dancers as a three-part Round.

# Appendices

## APPENDIX A

## STEP PATTERNS

These Sequences are often called "steps" and have a distinguishing name.

### WALTZ STEP OR WALTZ CLOG STEP

| COUNT | DESCRIPTION | | COUNT | DESCRIPTION |
|---|---|---|---|---|
| 1 | Step L | or | & 1 | Flap L to L |
| & 2 | Shuffle R | | & 2 | Shuffle R |
| & 3 | Ball-Change R-L | | & 3 | Ball-Change R-L |

### BUFFALO (moves to side R or L)

| COUNT | DESCRIPTION |
|---|---|
| 4 | Leap to R with R toe pointing to R (leg well turned out) |
| & a | Shuffle L to L side |
| 1 | Step L (L leg well turned out) and lift R foot up in front of L leg midway between knees and ankle, R toe pointed sharply down. R knee will be pointing R in line of direction and sole of R foot will be facing L. |

### PATRICOLA (good for use in a Soft Shoe)

| COUNT | DESCRIPTION | | COUNT | DESCRIPTION |
|---|---|---|---|---|
| 4 | Hop L | | a 3 | Flap R over L |
| & a | Shuffle R in front of L | | 4 | Hop R |
| 1 | Step R over L | | & a | Shuffle L in front of R |
| a 2 | Flap L to L | | 1 | Step L over R |

**43**

| | | | | |
|---|---|---|---|---|
| a 2 | Flap R to R | | a 3 | Flap R over L |
| a 3 | Flap L over R | | a 4 | Flap L to L |
| 4 | Hop L | | a 1 | Flap R over L |
| & a | Shuffle R over L | | a 2 | Flap L to L |
| 1 | Step R over L | | a 3 | Flap R over L |
| a 2 | Flap L to L | | | |

## TRAVEL (moves to side R or L)

| Count | Description | | Count | Description |
|---|---|---|---|---|
| 1 | Step L to L | | a 3 | Ball-Change R-L |
| a & | Shuffle R | | a & | Shuffle R |
| a 2 | Ball-Change R-L | | a 4 | Ball-Change R-L |
| a & | Shuffle R | | | |

## IRISH STEP

(This moves backward. It can also be done in place, turning, or moving forward by changing the direction of the step on counts 1 and 3. A Heel Drop may be substituted for the Hop.)

| Count | Description | | Count | Description |
|---|---|---|---|---|
| & 4 | Shuffle R in front of L | | & 2 | Shuffle L in front of R |
| & | Hop L | | & | Hop R |
| 1 | Step R moving back | | 3 | Step L moving back |

## SINGLE-TIME STEP

| Count | Description |
|---|---|
| 4 & | Shuffle L bringing L foot back of R |
| 1 | Hop R |
| 2 | Step L beside R |
| a 3 | Flap R slightly forward |
| & | Step L in place |

## DOUBLE-TIME STEP (Add 2 sounds on count 2.)

| Count | Description |
|---|---|
| 4 & | Shuffle L bringing L foot back of R |
| 1 | Hop R |
| & 2 | Flap L beside R |
| a 3 | Flap R slightly forward |
| & | Step L in place |

## TRIPLE-TIME STEP (Add 3 sounds on count 2.)

| Count | Description |
|---|---|
| 4 & | Shuffle L bringing L foot back of R |
| 1 | Hop R |

**44**

& a   Shuffle L to L side
2   Step L
a 3   Flap R slightly forward
&   Step L in place

## STAMP-TIME STEP

COUNT DESCRIPTION

1   Stamp R slightly in front of L
&   Pick-Up with R toe
2   Hop L
& 3   Flap R beside L
a 4   Flap L slightly forward
&   Step R in place

## APPENDIX B

### DANCE IN WALTZ TIME

3/4 WALTZ   MODERATE TEMPO   32 MEASURES   FOR BEGINNERS

| | | COUNT | DESCRIPTION | | COUNT | DESCRIPTION |
|---|---|---|---|---|---|---|
| PART I. | A. | 1 | Step L (waltz step) | C. | 1-3 1-3 | Repeat A |
| | | & 2 | Shuffle R | D. | 1 | Step forward on L heel |
| | | & 3 | Ball-change R-L | | 2 | Step forward on R heel |
| | | 1-3 | Repeat R | | 3 | Step back L |
| | B. | 1 | Step L | | 1 | Step back R |
| | | 2 | Brush R to L | | (2 3) | Hold |
| | | 3 | Hop L | | | |
| | | 1-3 | Repeat R | | | |

| | | COUNT | DESCRIPTION | | COUNT | DESCRIPTION |
|---|---|---|---|---|---|---|
| II. | A. | 1-3 1-3 | Repeat I A | C. | 1-3 1-3 | Repeat A |
| | B. | 1 | Step L | D. | 1-3 1-3 | Repeat I D |
| | | 2 | Touch R toe behind L heel | | | |
| | | 3 | Hop L | | | |
| | | 1-3 | Repeat (Make a full turn L during B) | | | |

| Count | Description | | Count | Description |
|-------|-------------|---|-------|-------------|
| III. A. 1-3 | Repeat I A | | C. 1-3 | Repeat A |
| 1-3 | | | 1-3 | |
| B. 1 | Step L over R | | D. 1-3 | Repeat I D |
| 2 | Pull L | | 1-3 | |
| 3 | Step R | | | |
| 1 | Step L | | | |
| & 2 | Shuffle R | | | |
| & | Hop L | | | |
| 3 | Step R | | | |

| Count | Description | | Count | Description |
|-------|-------------|---|-------|-------------|
| IV. A. 1-3 | Repeat I A | | C. 1-3 | Repeat A |
| 1-3 | | | 1-3 | |
| B. 1 | Step L | | D. 1 | Jump forward |
| 2 | Brush R to L | | 2 | Step back L |
| and | | | 3 | Step back R |
| (3) | Circle R over to R | | 1 | Step forward L |
| 1 | Place R heel to R | | 2 | Brush R |
| 2 | Toe Snap R | | 3 | Heel Drop L |
| (3) | Hold | | | |

# APPENDIX C

## SOURCES OF MATERIALS

### TAPS AND SHOES

CAPEZIO
1855 Broadway
New York, New York 10023

HERBET DANCEWEAR
1657 Broadway
New York, N.Y. 10019

SELVA and SONS, INC.
1607 Broadway
New York, N.Y. 10019

Also Dance-Theater Retail Shops in Boston, Chicago, Los Angeles, Hollywood, San Francisco, and San Mateo.

### RECORDS

HOCTOR DANCE RECORDS, INC.
Waldwick, N.J. 07473

Leo's
32 West Randolph St.
Chicago, Ill. 60601

Russell Records
Box 3318
Ventura, Calif. 90303

S & R Records
Selva and Sons, Inc.
1607 Broadway
New York, N. Y. 10019

## INFORMATION

Dance Magazine (268 West 47th St., New York, N. Y. 10036)
A monthly periodical with articles indexed in the *Reader's Guide to Periodical Literature;* runs a series of articles on tap techniques or dances; has a "Shopping Guide" which lists the magazine's advertisers by category: Dance Costumes, Footwear and Accessories, Records and Record Players, and the like.

The Dance Mart (Box 48 Homecrest Station, Brooklyn, N. Y. 11229) Sends out bibliographies of their available material; includes tap books in their listings.

Hungerford, Mary Jane, *Creative Tap Dancing*, New York: Prentice-Hall, Inc., 1939. Has a good chapter on tap history; includes analysis of form, recording dances, dances, values, and equipment.

Little, Elise A., "History of Tap," *The Dance Encyclopedia*, Anatole Chujoy, ed. New York: A. S. Barnes & Co., Inc., 1949. Pp. 464-468. Concise account of the important influences on the development of tap.

Sautoff, Hermine, *Tap Dance for Fun*, New York: A. S. Barnes & Co., Inc., 1941. A collection of dances with careful descriptions of rhythmic and movement patterns.

Winter, Marian Hannah, "Juba and American Minstrelsy," *Chronicles of the American Dance*, Paul Magriel, ed. New York: Henry Holt and Co., 1948. Pp. 39-63. Excellent account with illustrations of early days of minstrelsy.

## APPENDX D
## RECORD YOUR DANCES

Title _____

Music _____

Meter _____          Floor  pattern

Tempo _____

Number  of  measures _____

Number  of  dancers  _____

PART I.  A

## APPENDX D
## RECORD YOUR DANCES

Title _____

Music _____

Meter _____        Floor pattern

Tempo _____

Number of measures _____

Number of dancers _____

PART I.  A

## APPENDX D
## RECORD YOUR DANCES

Title _____

Music _____

Meter _____          Floor pattern

Tempo _____

Number of measures _____

Number of dancers _____

PART I.   A

## APPENDX D
## RECORD YOUR DANCES

Title _____

Music _____

Meter _____         Floor pattern

Tempo _____

Number of measures _____

Number of dancers _____

Part I.  A

# Index

## INDEX